I0152312

Out Of Winter
A Collection Of Poetry

Out Of Winter
A Collection Of Poetry
By: Rosalee Laws

Dedicated to my mom who is one of the kindest and most giving people I know. Also, to all of my friends, I do not know what I would have done without you the past year. And to Adam who encourages me everyday to be the person I can and am.

Out Of Winter

Contents

Introduction 5

Part One Chaos 7

Part Two Frozen 23

Part Three Melted 37

Rosalee Laws

Introduction

*Rosalee Laws, pursuing many arts of life, did no
different in this book of poetry. Crafting her
thoughts into a mosaic of words, she elegantly
brings you into her mind.
You will find yourself launched into a world of
emotion and introspection. Intertwining her
knowledge of human psychology, you will take
pleasure in a logical flow that mimics life and
reminds you of the trials and tribulations every
one goes through in their journey.
Her poetry offers a way to break free of the
daily superficiality you may get caught up in,
and view the world on another level. What you
read may bring tears to your eyes while
associating these words and feelings with your
own life experiences. These words are alive.
Chaos – frozen - melted.
~Jonathan Sorber*

Rosalee Laws

Part One
Chaos

Time

In a rush.
Left behind.
No pauses,
No breaths.
Lost and not.
No time.

Peace

I shall find no peace tonight.
Nor the perfect words to write.
I try to catch them,
Before they fly out of my head.
Trying to remember,
Before I forget what was said.
Circular thinking.
Going nowhere.
Peer into my soul,
Maybe I will find my peace there.

Goodbye

Goodbye she said.
Tomorrow I will be no longer.
But let the emptiness make you
Stronger.
Do not shed a tear.
Just feel the sun.
Remember I once felt the warmth on
My face,
But I shall miss the feeling of this place.
The colors.
The sounds,
The senses drink.
But feel love, generosity, and devotion.
Through them I will always be.

Bewilderment

The poison I intentionally drink.
A veil I succumb to.
Bewilderment engulfs me.
As a pattern sounds.
Listening is optional.
To live in dark or light,
Or to be in between?
To not know where to rest.
A prolonged blink,
May seem simple and familiar.

I Made You Laugh

I made you laugh.
You said I made you free.
You needed someone else,
And that someone was not me.
Should I have made myself something
Else?
No that is not how it should be,
I will not change myself purposely.
I should not have to try.
I made you laugh,
You made me cry.

Rose

Peak into my heart,
See what is inside.
Read the pages,
Where I reside.
My thoughts,
My hopes, my fears,
My woes.
Feel the thorns,
Smell the scent,
Of this withered rose.

Fall

I put you up high,
Only to fall myself.
The image could not live,
I only punished myself.
My thoughts only tortured me.
You were in a different world of
Thought,
Somewhere where I was not.
I was a fool.
I only burned me, when I thought it was
You.

Stars

Sources of light from the heavens above,
Shine down through the night to
Welcome my love.
Some do not concern themselves with stars,
To them, they seem so far.
But I see the beauty of their illumination.
For me, they hold pure fascination.
Through them we see the past,
As if it continued to last.
Just as I do, stars go through their lives,
Changing, taking on different colors,
And then they die.
Pure creation,
Then elimination.

Hell

Do I believe in hell?
No.
No other dimension of fire and
Brimstone at least.
We can choose to be in hell
Right now,
Here on earth,
Or we can release ourselves.
From our minds that seem to make us
Live in hell.
Watch the thinkers inside our heads,
Laugh when it throws in those
Preconditioned thoughts, of interpreting
now.
We choose and can create where we
want to be.

Me As My Creation

I try different ways of being,
So I can eliminate what I do not want
To be.
Keep what I need.
I wear different clothes,
To see what does not fit
Some people say to be self centered is wrong.
But how can we create and love others,
Without love of ourselves,
Or calculate where we belong?
We are responsible only for our own souls.
How we wish to evolve.
What we want to create.

Black Ties

Black ties,
Together like Velcro,
Pull apart.
No bond.
No heart.
No eternity.
Just a few mirage moments,
That resemble Memory.

Harsh Reality

My balance is weakened,
Pain rushes through,
Weariness takes me,
The chance I shall dance no more?
I may loose the ability to stand.
Or hold this pen in my hand.
Would I be any less?
Would it still be me?
If I am to succumb to that reality.

To Run Wild

A time where I do not have to run.
No place to run to.
To swing in the breeze,
Free of thought.
In control of what is going on in my
Head.
Free of judgment.
Suspended emotion.
To further in soul evolution.

Out Of Winter

Rosalee Laws

Part Two
Frozen

Not

NOT beautiful.
NOT desired.
NOT amazing.
NOT fun.
NOT lovable.
NOT hot like fire.
NOT the one.
Just NOT enough.

Opposite Reaction

*I'll grab ten, when I can only carry
Three.
Say yes, when I mean no.
Smile even when I hurt inside.
I keep busy so no one knows.
Rushing around, making precious
Moments A means to an end
These moments are lost, I can never
Have them again.*

Masks

Many faces,
Some Dark,
Some Light.
Some may say one is wrong,
One is right.
But they have blurred.
Bled into each other.
Separation is no longer possible,
Or Recognizable.

Pleasure and Pain

Feel the pain.
For without comes no joy.
Feel the razor.
Touch the satin.
Acknowledge the scrape.
Get engulfed by the silk.
Bleed.
But still breathe.

Yesterday Is Dead

Yesterday is dead.
Do not dwell on what has past in your
Words
Or in your head.
These are things I have already heard,
Events that can not change,
To try and relive yesterday, today, is
Absurd.
Those were my mistakes,
As bad as they may be,
But they have become a part of me.
You want it redone,
Something I cannot undo,
Even though I am sorry what I did hurt
You.

Pleasure Vs. Joy

Pleasure I gather from
OUTSIDE myself.
Joy I find
WITHIN myself.
Pleasure can turn into
Pain.
Pure joy can not
Change.
I would surpass the pleasure.

Where Is My Color?

My heart is turned to
Black.
My sky turned to
Gray.
How do I get my colors back?
At least I know the color is somewhere.

Stand Or Choose?

Do we leave the problems to be
Solved?
Or is the opposite true,
Will the universe reveal the answer?
Or is it entirely up to you?
Here lies the paradigm
That I often face.
Will a solution come at a future time
And space?
Just suddenly appear
Or is the real answer....you will never
Get anywhere.
Standing motionless, right here.
Nothing comes from nothing.
But my world is meant to unfold.
Do I make a quick decision?
Or do I hold?

Rosalee Laws

Imagination

Trying to grasp a phantom,
My hands remain empty
Because there is no substance really
There.
I have the illusion of sense
But it is an imaginary apparition
That I talk to and hear.

Wants

I offer you silver,
And you chose gold.
I clutch.
You shake off my grip.
I offer warmth,
You prefer the cold.
I gave you the gold.
I let go.
I let you feel the cold.
You wanted my silver.

Inspiration

Inspiration is plenty.
Motivation shines then hides.
Never wanted to be another,
Despite illusions of motionlessness.
To loop in thought and action,
Living only by reaction.
Where is the force to drive thought?
Where is the thought
To manifest reality?
A signal seems to be there
Then interrupted by itself.

Snuff

You have drained my life,
Exhausted my light,
Left me
To a cold night.
Left underneath you,
Frozen where you were.
I long to be free.
To find that spark that could be me.
Is there an effect,
Or just a reminiscence of us?
To be able to erase the dust.
Soiled with sting.
Motionless.

Rosalee Laws

Ice Reflection

I can go up,
Or I can descend.
It is my choice.
Ice reflection,
Warm rays,
Buried in the sand,
Or soar in the sky.
Low or high?
Is there an in between?

Part Three
Melted

Warmth Of Unknown

*There will always be some cold in the
Shadow of the sun,
But pay most attention to the small
Warm spots that come.
Too long have I dwelled in winter
Even though I love the snow,
It is time for spring to come
And to let the winter go.
There is no need, but only an
Enrichment of another.
So absorb the joy the closeness fathers.
You find happiness in the vicinity of a
Certain space,
Occupied by the warmth of a certain
Embrace.
Do not fall back into the prediction of
Now,*

Let the moment be what it will.
If those moments eventually fade
Away,
Be comforted by the memories,
Warmth, and happiness you had that
Day.

Universal Recognition

You hide inside,
Till no space remains.
Hiding and remaining,
Leaves things unchanged.
No choice at all,
Is a decision.
Even if it is to stay in
Your own prison.
An unknown source to draw you out.
A lesson from the unknown appears.
Peace coexists with tears.
Glimpses of a new perspective.
Patterns can now be reflected.
Simple yet intricate selfishness.
Balanced with pure selflessness.

Suspension

Learn to be lonely,
Only then will you not be alone.
What you think good,
What you think unfriendly,
Turn to bad,
May turn to great.
Oppose judgment,
For a moment.
Words are only symbols that point.
Some unknown end.

Choices

I have some choices to make,
I guess it's better than no choice at all.
I have run away,
And each time, I fall.
By making no choice,
I have made it.
It is just letting go of the reins,
But now I choose to capture them
Again.

Opposites

I go through hell to find the joy.
I experience what I do not want,
So I may find what I do.
I have created what I detest,
And may choose to destroy it.
There are no victims or villains
There is nothing I do not know,
Although I may forget.

Rosalee Laws

Unbound

The wind you feel but can not grasp.
The water that changes and ever flows.
The rainbow that cannot be caught.
The fire that cannot be touched.
I am the wind.
I am the water.
I am the rainbow.
I am the fire.
I just want to be free.
No one can hold onto me.

Lost In Me

Thou seek pleasure and palaces.
Across the lands you roam.
But thou seekest what thou can find at
Home.
For glitter dims and silvers fade,
So shall thou seeking fade away.
For thou shall find in me, the most
Luxurious gold.
All that is required is my hand to hold.
Treasures of passions freed,
Be entranced and awaken lost in me.

Rosalee Laws

About the Author

Rosalee Laws is a Renaissance soul with a poet's heart. Striving for creativity in all that she does, Rosalee has been an actor, a singer, a photographer, a model, and a secret agent. She currently resides in New York City.

www.ingramcontent.com/pod-product-compliance
Lightning Source LLC
LaVergne TN
LVHW091210080426
835509LV00006B/925